Changing States
25 Guided Imagery Scripts for Individual and Group Work

Copyright ©2016 by Stephanie L. Bolton

All rights reserved. No part of this book may be used or reproduced by any means, graphic, electronic, or mechanical, including photocopying, recording, taping or by any information storage retrieval system without the written permission of the author except in the case of brief quotations embodied in critical articles and reviews.

Table of Contents

Introduction		1
Chapter 1	The Who, What, and Why	2
Chapter 2	The How	4
Chapter 3	The Scripts and Their Use	8

- Centering/Relaxation — 13
  - Energy in Your Body — 14
  - Body Infused with Light — 16
  - Walk in the Countryside — 18
  - Field of Flowers — 20
  - Butterflies — 22
  - Mountain Hike — 24
  - Waterfall — 26
  - Porch Rocking Chair — 28
  - Maple Tree — 30
  - Rain Shower — 32
  - Stained Glass Window — 34
  - Boat Ride — 36
- Problem Solving — 39
  - Tree Roots — 40
  - Children's Playground — 42
  - Blowing Bubbles — 44
  - Building a Fence — 46
  - Redecorating a House — 48
  - Rainbow — 50
  - Magic Water Fountain — 52
- Deeper Wisdom — 57
  - Riverbank with Rocks — 58
  - Messages on Stones — 60
  - Decluttering the Attic — 62
  - Inner Wisdom — 64
  - Treasure Box — 66
  - Wise Person — 68

Music Suggestions	70
Creative Adaptations for Sessions	72
Resources	74

Introduction

After *Diving Deeper: 30 Guided Visualization Scripts for Individual and Group Work* was published in 2015, several readers wrote to me with wonderful feedback. One of the topics most suggested by them was a list of group activities that could be incorporated into the imagery experience. With that in mind, I have added a separate section at the end of this book with a list of in-depth questions and creative activities that can be used to extend and deepen the imagery experience for groups or individual participants. These questions and activities are intended to be open-ended and broad to allow for your creativity as the group leader as well as the creativity of your participants to tap into their inner wisdom and self-expression. Take them as suggestions and adapt as needed to fit your space, group intent, needs, etc.

Additionally, if you have read my first book, then you can skim or skip altogether the next few chapters. The information included in them is largely the same as that included in my first book, but I felt the need to include it here in case some readers were new and/or needed a refresher. The chapters have been slightly revised and updated, but the basic ideas remain the same.

Chapter One

The Who, What, and Why

This book was inspired by people- students, clinicians, clients, fellow therapists- asking me after guided meditation sessions where I found the visualization scripts I used. Enough people asked that I finally decided it was time to collect my original scripts and put them all in one place.

As a music therapist with a private practice in Guided Imagery and Music (GIM), I've led countless individual and group sessions using the scripts contained in this book. Before we go any further, it is important to distinguish between traditional GIM as conceived and developed by Helen Bonny and music assisted relaxation/imagery. The Bonny Method of GIM is characterized by pre-recorded, primarily classical, music programs played for an individual with the therapist (also called the 'guide') present to support and facilitate the imagery that is evoked by the music. Music assisted relaxation/imagery is characterized by pre-recorded music (not strictly limited to classical selections) of much shorter duration played for a group with the therapist actively directing the relaxation or imagery that occurs for the group members. The primary differences between the two are the therapist's involvement in the imagery process (no suggestions at all vs. suggesting it) and the number of people participating (individual vs. group). The use of these visualization scripts falls squarely into the category of music assisted relaxation/imagery.

These scripts are appropriate for use with individuals as well as small to medium size groups (12-14 maximum). I have found them useful in introducing the imagery process to individuals who are new to GIM sessions. The scripts have also been helpful for individuals wanting to enhance their meditation or mindfulness practice as they provide a 'change of scenery' to the usual routine. In group settings, they offer a way for group members to connect with themselves and other group participants on a deeper level as well as experience the group's topic or theme that day in a different way.

This book is intended for use by music therapists as well as other related counseling professionals and healthcare workers. Experienced support group leaders and wellness group facilitators may also discover useful ideas for their meetings here, especially in the first few sections of scripts.

A word of caution here: as people working in the helping professions, we know that emotionally significant material can surface at any time, and sometimes without much warning or provocation. These visualization scripts begin by scratching the surface of our life experience and progress to diving deeper into subconscious material. Be mindful of your clients' and/or group members' lives and experiences, and take that knowledge into consideration when planning to use these scripts. A colleague of mine used to say, "Keep the lid on the can of worms—unless you know how to manage a room full of worms!" Dealing with individuals' mental and emotional health issues can be difficult work, and advanced training and education are strongly recommended.

Chapter Two

The How

It's not as easy as it looks to lead a group through a guided visualization experience. First, you need to choose an appropriate music selection that corresponds with the group's intent that day as well as their overall energy level. The length of the music also needs to be considered. Having the music come to completion a minute before you finish the script can ruin an experience! Your tone of voice, pace of speaking, inflections, pauses—it all works together to create a meaningful experience for participants. So let's discuss those topics in a little more detail.

The Voice: The volume at which you speak during the visualization exercise needs to be loud enough that all participants can easily hear you (straining to hear the speaker can be terribly distracting!) but not so loud that your voice disrupts their ability to concentrate on what is happening internally for them. Enunciation is also important here; speak clearly and distinctly using the mid-range register of your voice. Pacing is another key element. Going too fast, or too slow, can inhibit participants from having a deep and meaningful experience. Although indications for pausing in the scripts have been included, consider them merely suggestions for you. Base your pauses on the group's energy level and your own intuition about how long you need to remain silent. It will also depend on what is happening in the script as well. You would likely want a longer pause when instructing the group to ponder what they find within the treasure box compared to noticing what they see or hear by a waterfall. Use your best judgment and allow yourself to adjust over time—facilitating a visualization becomes easier the more you practice and do it.

The Music: Choosing the music is a significant part of a guided visualization exercise. You will need to consider several factors when selecting a piece (or pieces) to use—length, instrumentation, tempo, mood, and expansiveness. We will take these one at a time:

- Length-- The best option is to time yourself while practicing a script and determine how long it takes you to go through it (include the pauses!), then use that timeframe to choose music that runs that length. For example, if a particular script takes you 8 minutes to read through, then you will look for a piece of music that lasts roughly 8 minutes. When choosing a piece, it is best to err on the side of the music being slightly longer than what you need. Participants will be more likely to notice the music ending before you do than they will if it runs 30 seconds too long. Additionally, you always have the option of fading the music out near the end if you realize you have a considerable amount of time left (i.e., more than 30 seconds).
- Instrumentation-- For the purposes of these visualization scripts and group experiences, you will want to choose music that involves fewer instruments. For example, solo piano or guitar arrangements with another instrument filling in the background are good choices. Woodwind and string instruments are best here; brass and percussion tend to be too bright and/or jarring for these experiences. In most cases, background environmental sounds (e.g., rainfall, ocean waves, birds chirping) should be avoided. The exceptions to that might be for those scripts that specifically mention those sounds, but be aware that they might be distracting to group participants. If you decide to use more than one piece of music for a script, be sure that all the pieces are of similar instrumentation so they flow together nicely for the participants. It can be distracting to participants to begin an experience with solo piano but then hear saxophone halfway through the script. Music with lyrics, even if they are a foreign language, should be avoided. Participants need to be focusing on your voice, not trying to discern between what you are saying and what another voice is doing on the music recording.

- Tempo-- The tempo of the chosen music should fall in the range of 50-80 beats per minute. If you are not musically trained, that translates to about one beat per second. Essentially, the music needs to be slow enough to induce a relaxed state of mind for participants, but not so slow that they become drowsy and have to resist sleep. If you are using music that has multiple instruments, make sure that one instrument is not playing significantly faster than another (e.g., one plays long sustained notes while another plays a series of repetitive runs up and down the scale).
- Mood-- When choosing music to go along with a script, consider the mood of the script first. Is it uplifting or introspective, lighthearted or more emotional? Try to select music that matches the particular mood of the script.
- Expansiveness-- The term 'container' is sometimes used in describing supportive, therapeutic meetings or sessions. It denotes the physical and emotional space required for the group or individual in that setting. The first section of scripts could be described as small 'containers' because they do not involve deep, emotional experiences on the part of the participants. The rest of the scripts could be considered slightly larger 'containers' because they involve more inner, emotional work. When choosing music, keep in mind the size of your 'container.' For small 'containers,' you will want to choose music that has very few instruments and is fairly predictable in how it sounds. Simple melodies with one or two instruments are best here. For the slightly larger 'containers,' you can select music that involves a few more instruments with moderately complex melodies.

If you have not experienced a Level I GIM training, then I would strongly recommend it. In the training you will learn how to listen to music in a new way as well as gain experience guiding a group/individual and being guided by someone else.

The best suggestion I can make is to have a dress rehearsal of your own with the music and the script. Read through it, see how it feels, determine if the music and script match up well, play around with the pauses and the overall pacing. Take your cues from the participants, and be compassionate with yourself during this process. Inevitably, something will not go as planned or a participant will have a negative reaction—consider it 'grist for the mill' when you debrief the experience afterwards. Most importantly, enjoy the journey and the experience!

Chapter Three

The Scripts

The visualization scripts have been divided into three sections. The first section generally stays 'on the surface' of life experience. These scripts do not require the individual to dig into deeply personal issues, dredge up repressed memories, or unearth significant emotional material. These scripts are intended to be primarily shallow and allow the participant to get in touch with their physical body, practice relaxation, and create a few personal visualization scenes that can be revisited again and again for the purposes of stress relief or gentle meditation. The scripts in this beginning section does not require the participant to analyze their experience much beyond determining "how well did this work for me?"

The remaining sections of scripts should be used by those trained in navigating the deeper waters of the subconscious. They were crafted in a way that encourages and allows the participant to be open and receptive to profound self-knowledge and wisdom. The handling and processing of that information in a group or individual setting requires appropriate education and experience, and it should be taken seriously. These scripts are intended for use after trust and rapport have been established between therapist/facilitator and participant (or group).

Preparation for Use

Whether using these scripts for a group meeting or individual session, make certain that there will be no distractions or interruptions during the session time. There are few things worse than being halfway through a visualization exercise only to have another person unknowingly come barging into the room and ruin the moment! Take the necessary precautions to limit outside noise, distractions, and interruptions. Double check that your equipment is working correctly and that any electronic devices are fully charged and set to the appropriate settings. Remember to check the volume level of the speaker or stereo system as well.

Depending on the office or meeting room area you will be using, have some cushions, pillows, yoga mats, and small blankets available for participants to make themselves more comfortable—or suggest they bring their own if you know ahead of time that you will be incorporating a visualization exercise that day. Laying on a hard floor or sitting in an uncomfortable office chair can be counterproductive when trying to imagine oneself in a favorite place!

Suggestions for Use

Centering/Relaxation: These are useful for participants who are new to the imagery process. They are geared towards general relaxation and simply being present in the moment. Excellent to use if you want to introduce mindfulness practice to the group/individual. Also helpful in grounding individuals after an especially emotional therapy session. Some of these scripts expand on the imagery experience and incorporate additional sensory information (sights, smells, sounds, etc.).

Problem Solving: These scripts can be used to help participants become aware of the many ways that problems can be solved—a way of opening their eyes to 'out of the box' thinking. It can also point out areas where they may struggle with critical thinking skills and how to manage those situations as well. Allow extra time for processing these experiences.

Deeper Wisdom: These scripts should only be used by experienced facilitators and participants as they are the most in-depth experiences. Many of these scripts are very similar to the previously used scripts, only with slight modifications to allow for a deeper experience. This can be useful, especially if the participants are familiar with the previous scripts. Allow extra time for processing these experiences.

Additional Considerations

In addition to the cautions mentioned above, there are a few other important items to consider when using these visualization scripts.

Setting: What will the room environment be like where the group/individual will be? Is it fully enclosed, or will other people be able to walk by/peek inside/pass through/etc.? Will you be able to control for external sounds (e.g., overhead announcements, noisy hallway conversations)? How is the room arranged? Are there adequate comfortable chairs and/or places to recline or lay down? Do you have access to a thermostat, space heater, or fan? Depending on the specifics of each situation, there may be limits to what one can control. However, to ensure the best quality experience for participants, it is advised to address as many of these issues as possible.

Support: What support will be available? Will you lead on your own or have a co-facilitator or other staff present to help? If co-leading, will you debrief afterwards? Are you seeking professional supervision (peer and/or individual) to deal with any issues/situations that might arise?

Diagnosis: As mentioned several times previously, these visualization scripts are intended to improve general wellness and help manage stress. They are *not* recommended for those individuals experiencing active psychosis, hallucinations, delusions, significant confusion, or inability to differentiate between reality and imagination. Participants should be able to focus for a minimum of 20 minutes in order to be able to fully benefit from these scripts. Those who are suffering from significant cognitive deficits or extreme low energy (perhaps due to severe depression) may have some difficulty with these exercises.

Centering/Relaxation Scripts

Energy in Your Body

Close your eyes and take some deep breaths. Feel your lungs expanding with each inhale and contracting with each exhale. Feel your body open up with each new breath. Feel your muscles relax, all tension from the day leaving your body and mind. Notice that your mind becomes calmer and uncluttered with worry. With each deep breath feel yourself deepening further into quiet, alert relaxation. (pause for a few seconds)

Become aware of how it feels to breathe in…. and out…. (pause) notice if the air changes temperature slightly as you inhale and exhale… pay attention to the smallest detail… (pause) now bringing your attention to how the air fills your lungs… and leaves your lungs…. (pause) notice how your body changes slightly to accommodate each inhale… and exhale… how your chest expands… how your belly expands… and how they relax… (pause) until you're fully… deeply… effortlessly breathing… (pause)

Now thinking of your breath as energy, breathe it in even more deeply…. Deeply into the core of your being… (pause) notice where you feel that energy…. Be aware of how it feels… (pause) gently begin to move that energy throughout your body… feel each part of your body energize and tingle slightly as the energy expands… (pause) notice how you feel warm and alive as the energy travels around your body… (pause) This energy is always available to you… every time you breathe… every time you pause… every time you focus on feeling it… (pause)

Slowly and gradually allow the warmth and tingling sensations to fade… allow the energy to lessen… until you feel it only in the core of your being… (pause) knowing that it's always here and can be activated whenever you wish… (pause) and gently bring your attention back to your breath. Feeling the deep inhale, exhale…. Inhale, exhale. Noticing how calm and relaxed your body feels sitting here in this room. Gently open your awareness to this time and place, these surroundings... wiggle your fingers and toes, gently begin to move your body again.... and when you're ready, you can open your eyes.

Body Infused with Light

Close your eyes and take some deep breaths. Feel your lungs expanding with each inhale and contracting with each exhale. Feel your body open up with each new breath. Feel your muscles relax, all tension from the day leaving your body and mind. Notice that your mind becomes calmer and uncluttered with worry. With each deep breath feel yourself deepening further into quiet, alert relaxation. (pause for a few seconds)

Become aware of how it feels to breathe in…. and out…. (pause) notice if the air changes temperature slightly as you inhale and exhale… pay attention to the smallest detail… (pause) now bringing your attention to how the air fills your lungs… and leaves your lungs…. (pause) notice how your body changes slightly to accommodate each inhale… and exhale… how your chest expands… how your belly expands… and how they relax… (pause) until you're fully… deeply… effortlessly breathing… (pause)

Now thinking of your breath as a small ball of light, breathe it in even more deeply…. Deeply into the core of your being… (pause) the light can be any color you choose…. notice where you feel that light…. Be aware of how it feels… (pause) gently begin to move that light throughout your body… feel each part of your body energize and tingle slightly as the light expands… (pause) notice how you feel warm and alive as the light travels around your body… (pause) until your entire being is filled with this light… (pause) This light and energy is always available to you… every time you breathe… every time you pause… every time you focus on feeling it… (pause)

Slowly and gradually allow the warmth and tingling sensations to fade… allow the light to lessen… until you feel it only in the core of your being… (pause) knowing that it's always here and can be activated whenever you wish… (pause) and gently bring your attention back to your breath. Feeling the deep inhale, exhale…. Inhale, exhale. Noticing how calm and relaxed your body feels sitting here in this room. Gently open your awareness to this time and place, these surroundings… wiggle your fingers and toes, gently begin to move your body again.... and when you're ready, you can open your eyes.

Walk in the Countryside

Close your eyes and take some deep breaths. Feel your lungs expanding with each inhale and contracting with each exhale. Feel your body open up with each new breath. Feel your muscles relax, all tension from the day leaving your body and mind. Notice that your mind becomes calmer and uncluttered with worry. With each deep breath feel yourself deepening further into quiet, alert relaxation.
(pause for a few seconds)

Now imagine that you're standing in the countryside.... Everything around you is lush and green.... There are hills as far as you can see.... beautiful green hills.... You can feel the sun warm on your face... the breeze gently blowing... notice how it feels against your skin... smell the scent of summer and grass in the air... hear the sounds of birds chirping nearby... be aware of how it feels to be in this place.... Peaceful... calm... relaxed.... carefree....

You begin to walk leisurely through the grass towards a hill nearby... you pass a patch of clover and pause for a moment to watch a few bees there... hearing them faintly buzzing.... Continuing on up the side of the hill your attention is drawn to a pair of yellow butterflies flitting nearby... the breeze grows stronger for a moment and carries them away as you reach the top of the hill... standing at the top of the hill you can see even farther.... Beautiful green all around.... Bright sunshine.... Vibrant blue skies.... A lovely view.... (long pause)

After several minutes of enjoying this place, you begin walking again... breathing the fresh air in deeply... hearing the sounds of nature all around you... feeling completely at ease and peaceful... appreciating this time spent here in the countryside... knowing that you can come back whenever you want to... (short pause)

Gently bring your attention back to your breath. Feeling the deep inhale, exhale.... Inhale, exhale. Noticing how calm and relaxed your body feels sitting here in this room. Gently open your awareness to this time and place, these surroundings… wiggle your fingers and toes, gently begin to move your body again…. and when you're ready, you can open your eyes.

Field of Flowers

Close your eyes and take some deep breaths. Feel your lungs expanding with each inhale and contracting with each exhale. Feel your body open up with each new breath. Feel your muscles relax, all tension from the day leaving your body and mind. Notice that your mind becomes calmer and uncluttered with worry. With each deep breath feel yourself deepening further into quiet, alert relaxation. (pause for a few seconds)

Now imagine that you're standing in a field of flowers…. Everything around you is lush and green…. There are flowers as far as you can see…. You can feel the sun warm on your face… the breeze gently blowing… notice how it feels against your skin… smell the scent of summer and flowers in the air… hear the sounds of birds chirping nearby… be aware of how it feels to be in this place…. Relaxed… Calm… Peaceful… carefree….

You begin to walk leisurely through the flowers… you pause for a moment to watch a few bees fly from flower to flower… hearing them faintly buzzing…. You notice a clearing ahead and decide to sit down for a few moments there… enjoying the beautiful flowers all around…. Bright sunshine…. Vibrant blue skies…. (short pause) Your attention is drawn to a flower nearby and you begin to study it… notice how it moves in the breeze… its color…. Its size and shape… all its variations…. (long pause)

After several minutes of enjoying this place, you stand up and begin walking back through the field… breathing the fresh air in deeply… hearing the sounds of nature all around you… feeling completely at ease and peaceful… appreciating this time spent here in the field… knowing that you can come back whenever you want to… (short pause)

Gently bring your attention back to your breath. Feeling the deep inhale, exhale…. Inhale, exhale. Noticing how calm and relaxed your body feels sitting here in this room. Gently open your awareness to this time and place, these surroundings... wiggle your fingers and toes, gently begin to move your body again.... and when you're ready, you can open your eyes.

Butterflies

Close your eyes and take some deep breaths. Feel your lungs expanding with each inhale and contracting with each exhale. Feel your body open up with each new breath. Feel your muscles relax, all tension from the day leaving your body and mind. Notice that your mind becomes calmer and uncluttered with worry. With each deep breath feel yourself deepening further into quiet, alert relaxation. (pause for a few seconds)

Now imagine that you're standing out in nature.... Everything around you is lush and green.... There are hills as far as you can see.... You can feel the sun warm on your face... the breeze gently blowing... notice how it feels against your skin... smell the scent of summer and grass in the air... hear the sounds of birds chirping nearby... be aware of how it feels to be in this place.... Relaxed... Peaceful... Carefree... calm...

You begin to walk leisurely along... you pass some flowers and pause for a moment to watch a few bees there... hearing them faintly buzzing.... Continuing along your attention is drawn to a pair of yellow butterflies flitting nearby... you stop for a moment to watch them... a few more butterflies join them... and then a few more.... All different kinds and different colors and sizes.... And soon you're standing in the midst of hundreds of butterflies.... You marvel at them.... Thinking of how delicate they are.... How small and yet so beautiful... amazed at how they transform themselves from caterpillars into these wonderful winged creatures.... (short pause)

After several moments of enjoying the butterflies, they begin to slowly fly away... you watch them drift off with the breeze... feeling so fortunate to have been here for this experience with them.... slowly you begin walking again... breathing the fresh air in deeply... hearing the sounds of nature all around you... feeling completely at ease and peaceful... appreciating this time spent here in the countryside... knowing that you can come back whenever you want to... thinking of the butterflies and their transformation... (short pause)

Gently bring your attention back to your breath. Feeling the deep inhale, exhale…. Inhale, exhale. Noticing how calm and relaxed your body feels sitting here in this room. Gently open your awareness to this time and place, these surroundings… wiggle your fingers and toes, gently begin to move your body again…. and when you're ready, you can open your eyes.

Mountain Hike

Close your eyes and take some deep breaths. Feel your lungs expanding with each inhale and contracting with each exhale. Feel your body open up with each new breath. Feel your muscles relax, all tension from the day leaving your body and mind. Notice that your mind becomes calmer and uncluttered with worry. With each deep breath feel yourself deepening further into quiet, alert relaxation. (pause for a few seconds)

Now imagine that you're standing out in nature…. Looking around, you notice that you're in the mountains…. You can smell the pine scent of forest trees… feel the sun warm on your face… the breeze gently blowing… notice how it feels against your skin… hear the sounds of birds chirping nearby… the sound of squirrels and chipmunks in the leaves… be aware of how it feels to be in this place…. Relaxed… Peaceful… Carefree… calm…

You notice a trail nearby and begin to walk leisurely along… it's a wide trail and looks well-traveled although you're the only one here now… you appreciate the time to yourself out here in the woods… free to take your time and enjoy nature as you wish…. No hurry… no rush… (short pause)

After several moments of walking, you begin to notice the nature sounds around you…. Leaves rustling on the forest floor as you walk… animals scurrying in the underbrush…. Birds overhead in the trees…. You think you hear the sound of water nearby and come upon a small creek…. There's a footbridge going over it so you walk to the middle and stand looking down at the water… watching it go underneath the bridge… noticing how clear it is… you can see the rocks on the creek bottom…. And tiny little fish…. (short pause)

You go back across the bridge the way you came… feeling refreshed and energized… appreciating the time you've spent hiking in the woods…. Continuing up the trail to where you started, noticing everything about the forest as you pass by…. (short pause)… inhaling deeply the scent of the woods... feeling the peace and calm... knowing you can come back here anytime you want.... (long pause)

Gently bring your attention back to your breath. Feeling the deep inhale, exhale.... Inhale, exhale. Noticing how calm and relaxed your body feels sitting here in this room. Gently open your awareness to this time and place, these surroundings... wiggle your fingers and toes, gently begin to move your body again.... and when you're ready, you can open your eyes.

Waterfall

Close your eyes and take some deep breaths. Feel your lungs expanding with each inhale and contracting with each exhale. Feel your body open up with each new breath. Feel your muscles relax, all tension from the day leaving your body and mind. Notice that your mind becomes calmer and uncluttered with worry. With each deep breath feel yourself deepening further into quiet, alert relaxation. (pause for a few seconds)

Now imagine that you're standing out in nature…. Looking around, you notice that you're in the mountains…. You can smell the pine scent of forest trees… feel the sun warm on your face… the breeze gently blowing… notice how it feels against your skin… hear the sounds of birds chirping nearby… the sound of squirrels and chipmunks in the leaves… be aware of how it feels to be in this place…. Relaxed… Peaceful… Carefree… calm…

You notice a trail nearby and begin to walk leisurely along… it's a wide trail and looks well-traveled although you're the only one here now… you appreciate the time to yourself out here in the woods… free to take your time and enjoy nature as you wish…. No hurry… no rush… (short pause)

After several moments of walking, you begin to notice the nature sounds around you…. Leaves rustling on the forest floor as you walk… animals scurrying in the underbrush…. Birds overhead in the trees…. You think you hear the sound of water nearby and come upon a large waterfall just around the next bend in the trail…. You stand there marveling at its beauty… letting the sound of the water fill your ears… feeling your skin become slightly damp from the spray… noticing how the air is cooler here…. (short pause)

You notice a flat rock nearby and sit down on it… enjoying this place… simply being with nature… watching the waterfall and the water flow nearby… no hurry…. No rush… just enjoying the peaceful time here… (long pause)

After awhile, you stand and go back along the trail the way you came... feeling refreshed and energized... appreciating the time you've spent hiking in the woods.... Continuing up the trail to where you started, noticing everything about the forest as you pass by.... (short pause)... inhaling deeply the scent of the woods... feeling the peace and calm... knowing you can come back here anytime you want.... (long pause)

Gently bring your attention back to your breath. Feeling the deep inhale, exhale.... Inhale, exhale. Noticing how calm and relaxed your body feels sitting here in this room. Gently open your awareness to this time and place, these surroundings... wiggle your fingers and toes, gently begin to move your body again.... and when you're ready, you can open your eyes.

Porch Rocking Chair

Close your eyes and take some deep breaths. Feel your lungs expanding with each inhale and contracting with each exhale. Feel your body open up with each new breath. Feel your muscles relax, all tension from the day leaving your body and mind. Notice that your mind becomes calmer and uncluttered with worry. With each deep breath feel yourself deepening further into quiet, alert relaxation. (pause for a few seconds)

Now imagine that you're standing in front of a door... see the door clearly in your mind... notice its' shape... the material it's made of... its' color... reach out to turn the doorknob and open the door.... On the other side you find a spacious porch... stepping through the door you look around and observe the surroundings... what do you see? (pause) Notice the temperature of the air.... The sounds you hear... does this place seem familiar, or is it new to you? Using all of your senses to experience this place... (pause)

Your attention is drawn to a rocking chair on the far end of the porch... walking over to it, you sit down and begin slowly rocking... back and forth... back and forth... feeling the gentle motion of the chair as it moves... how relaxing it feels to simply sit and rock.... Observing your surroundings on the porch... feeling comfortable here... simply watching what happens around you... enjoying this time to yourself to relax and be still.... (long pause)

After awhile you sense a shift in the temperature and realize that the day will be coming to a close soon... letting the rocking chair slowly stop moving... savoring these last few moments on the porch... (pause) Rising from the chair, you walk along the porch to the door... opening it back up... crossing over the threshold... bringing with you a deep sense of relaxation... peace... calm...

Gently bring your attention back to your breath. Feeling the deep inhale, exhale.... Inhale, exhale. Noticing how calm and relaxed your body feels

sitting here in this room. Gently open your awareness to this time and place, these surroundings... wiggle your fingers and toes, gently begin to move your body again.... and when you're ready, you can open your eyes.

Maple Tree

Close your eyes and take some deep breaths. Feel your lungs expanding with each inhale and contracting with each exhale. Feel your body open up with each new breath. Feel your muscles relax, all tension from the day leaving your body and mind. Notice that your mind becomes calmer and uncluttered with worry. With each deep breath feel yourself deepening further into quiet, alert relaxation. (pause for a few seconds)

Now imagine that you're walking outside in nature…. It can be anywhere you choose… a familiar place… or a new place…. Feel the temperature of the air around you… inhale deeply the scent of the outdoors… hear the sound of birds… notice the colors of everything around you… feel the ground beneath your feet… (pause) enjoy the feeling of not being rushed or hurried… knowing you can take as much time as you want here… (pause)

As you walk, you notice a short distance away a very large maple tree… full of leaves… standing majestically here… you stop and marvel at it… noticing how the leaves move gently in the breeze… hearing the sound of the wind pass through them… seeing birds fly around the tree… squirrels run up and down the trunk… (pause) And as you stand watching this amazing tree, you notice that the fullness of its' summer foliage is gradually shifting… the leaves begin to change colors for autumn…. Beautiful bright colors… and then they begin to fall… cascades of colors blowing around the tree…. Onto the ground… blanketing the space underneath the tree…. Until there are no leaves left and the tree limbs are bare for winter… resting… conserving energy… waiting… until spring buds begin to form… and the bright green leaves gradually grow out… the vibrant green of spring…. Fresh and alive again…. As they grow fuller and stronger into summer… and the cycle continues… (pause)

Feeling grateful that you could watch this amazing transformation… noticing what's changed around you… what's changed within you… the sun is setting… the breeze turns cooler… you walk the way you came…

feeling thankful for the time here today... for the walk... for the maple tree... for the beauty and rest and refreshment and reflection... (pause)

Gently bring your attention back to your breath. Feeling the deep inhale, exhale.... Inhale, exhale. Noticing how calm and relaxed your body feels sitting here in this room. Gently open your awareness to this time and place, these surroundings... wiggle your fingers and toes, gently begin to move your body again.... and when you're ready, you can open your eyes.

Rain Shower

Close your eyes and take some deep breaths. Feel your lungs expanding with each inhale and contracting with each exhale. Feel your body open up with each new breath. Feel your muscles relax, all tension from the day leaving your body and mind. Notice that your mind becomes calmer and uncluttered with worry. With each deep breath feel yourself deepening further into quiet, alert relaxation. (pause for a few seconds)

Now imagine that you're walking down a short path through the woods.... Notice the trees and plants around you... hear the sounds of birds nearby... see the vibrant colors of flowers blooming... feel the worn path beneath your feet... the temperature of the air against your skin... using all your senses to experience this walk in the woods... (pause)

As you inhale a deep breath of forest air, you notice the scent of rain... straining your ears you can just begin to hear the sound of raindrops hitting the leaves overhead... quietly and slowly at first... gradually gaining in frequency... until you're caught in a rain shower... (pause) noticing a large tree nearby, you jog over to take shelter under its' canopy... standing next to the massive trunk you look up into the branches and limbs... straight towards the top... watching as a few raindrops filter through and fall down... (pause)

Standing there next to the tree trunk, you imagine the rainwater nourishing the ground below... rejuvenating the plants and trees with its' nourishment.... giving them life... helping them grow.... refreshing everything here... (pause)

After awhile you hear the rain begin to slow down... you come out from beneath the canopy of the tree... feeling gratitude for its' shelter from the rain... stepping back onto the path... noticing what's changed around you... the sun is setting... the breeze turns cooler... you walk back down the path through the woods... feeling grateful for the time here today... for the rain... for the trees... for the rest and refreshment... (pause)

Gently bring your attention back to your breath. Feeling the deep inhale, exhale…. Inhale, exhale. Noticing how calm and relaxed your body feels sitting here in this room. Gently open your awareness to this time and place, these surroundings… wiggle your fingers and toes, gently begin to move your body again…. and when you're ready, you can open your eyes.

Stained Glass Window

Close your eyes and take some deep breaths. Feel your lungs expanding with each inhale and contracting with each exhale. Feel your body open up with each new breath. Feel your muscles relax, all tension from the day leaving your body and mind. Notice that your mind becomes calmer and uncluttered with worry. With each deep breath feel yourself deepening further into quiet, alert relaxation. (pause for a few seconds)

Now imagine that you're walking outside in nature…. It can be anywhere you choose… a familiar place… or a new place…. Feel the temperature of the air around you… inhale deeply the scent of the outdoors… hear the sound of birds… notice the colors of everything around you… feel the ground beneath your feet… (pause) enjoy the feeling of not being rushed or hurried… knowing you can take as much time as you want here… (pause)

As you walk, you notice a short distance away an old church… getting closer you see that it has a very large and beautiful stained glass window… wanting to see it better, you open the entry door of the church and go inside… noticing that you're alone inside the sanctuary… finding a seat with a good view of the window, you sit down… watching how the sunlight streams through the stained glass… all the many colors… the patterns… marveling at the craftsmanship that went into creating the window… paying close attention to all the details… (pause) enjoying the quiet here… feeling relaxed… peaceful… calm… (pause) simply watching the sunlight play in the colors… (pause)

Feeling grateful that you could enjoy this experience… noticing what's changed around you… what's changed within you… you stand up and leave the church… walking back the way you came… feeling thankful for the time here today… for the window… for the church… for the beauty and rest and refreshment and reflection… (pause)

Gently bring your attention back to your breath. Feeling the deep inhale, exhale.... Inhale, exhale. Noticing how calm and relaxed your body feels sitting here in this room. Gently open your awareness to this time and place, these surroundings... wiggle your fingers and toes, gently begin to move your body again.... and when you're ready, you can open your eyes.

Boat Ride

Close your eyes and take some deep breaths. Feel your lungs expanding with each inhale and contracting with each exhale. Feel your body open up with each new breath. Feel your muscles relax, all tension from the day leaving your body and mind. Notice that your mind becomes calmer and uncluttered with worry. With each deep breath feel yourself deepening further into quiet, alert relaxation. (pause for a few seconds)

Now imagine that you're standing on a dock near the water... at the end of the dock is a boat... you walk down the dock and toward the boat... using your senses to be aware of everything around you... the sights... the sounds... the smells... the temperature of the air... the sturdy wooden planks of the dock as you walk... (pause) notice the details of the boat itself... its' size... shape... color... how it moves gently in the water... (pause)

Now climbing carefully into the boat... you notice that it's steadier than you expected... and finding a place to sit down, you settle in... feeling safe and secure in the boat... knowing that it's sturdy enough for these waters... (pause) slowly the boat moves away from the dock... perhaps you are rowing the boat yourself... or the action of the water is causing the boat to drift with the current... or the wind is filling the sails... or by some force of magic the boat simply moves on its' own... whatever it is, you simply go along with it... feeling confident... and safe... and excited to be on this short journey... (pause) becoming aware of the gentle movement of the boat in the water... hearing the sounds of the waves against the boat... occasionally feeling water splash onto you... smelling the air... enjoying the scenery... noticing everything around you... (pause) feeling relaxed... refreshed... deeply contented... (long pause)

Now noticing that the boat is slowly making its' way back to the dock... you see it in the distance... getting closer... bringing these feelings of relaxation with you... and closer... letting the peace and calm sink in... until the boat gently bumps against the dock again... and carefully climbing out of the boat, you stand on the dock... feeling grateful that you could enjoy this experience... noticing what's changed around you... what's changed within you... you walk back up the dock the way you came... feeling thankful for the time here today... for the water... for the boat... for the beauty and rest and refreshment and reflection... (pause)

Gently bring your attention back to your breath. Feeling the deep inhale, exhale.... Inhale, exhale. Noticing how calm and relaxed your body feels sitting here in this room. Gently open your awareness to this time and place, these surroundings... wiggle your fingers and toes, gently begin to move your body again.... and when you're ready, you can open your eyes.

Problem Solving

Scripts

Tree Roots

Close your eyes and take some deep breaths. Feel your lungs expanding with each inhale and contracting with each exhale. Feel your body open up with each new breath. Feel your muscles relax, all tension from the day leaving your body and mind. Notice that your mind becomes calmer and uncluttered with worry. With each deep breath feel yourself deepening further into quiet, alert relaxation. (pause for a few seconds)

Now imagine that you're standing on a riverbank. Notice how the river looks.... is it a wide river or a smaller one... Is it running fast or slow... is the water clear or murky... deep or shallow.... can you see any fish swimming by.... Notice how the water moves.... Hear the sounds of the water gently lapping against the riverbank nearby.... Bring your attention to the trees and vegetation where you are...

One tree in particular draws your attention.... it's one of the larger trees on the riverbank and has numerous large and twisted roots... they spread for yards around the tree's base... some of these roots reach down to the water.... roots that have grown over and under each other for many, many years..... strong roots that support a massive tree.... You walk closer to the tree and start to climb around the roots.... After some time you notice that there is a bare earthy area between some of the roots closest to the river... you make your way over to that spot and decide to sit down amongst the roots.... It's a perfect fit for you....

You sit there amongst the roots for some time... feeling grounded in the earth... hands gently resting on the roots closest to you.... Feeling their strength.... Thinking how they bring up from the earth what the tree needs to grow and flourish.... Thinking how strong they are to support such a large tree... thinking of how old and wise this tree must be.... Wondering what you might learn from this tree.... From these twisted roots... from this river and how it flows.... You sit here for some time feeling deeply settled and breathing it all in....(long pause here)

Feeling like you've absorbed what you need from this experience with the tree, you begin to slowly rise from where you've been sitting…. you pause for a moment to send gratitude to the tree for its shelter and wisdom… carefully stepping your way out of the tree roots and back to the riverbank… you begin walking back the way you came… noticing if anything about your surroundings is different…. Notice if you feel different…. Thinking about what you've learned here today…. (short pause here)

Gently bring your attention back to your breath. Feeling the deep inhale, exhale…. Inhale, exhale. Noticing how calm and relaxed your body feels sitting here in this room. Gently open your awareness to this time and place, these surroundings… wiggle your fingers and toes, gently begin to move your body again…. and when you're ready, you can open your eyes.

Children's Playground

Close your eyes and take some deep breaths. Feel your lungs expanding with each inhale and contracting with each exhale. Feel your body open up with each new breath. Feel your muscles relax, all tension from the day leaving your body and mind. Notice that your mind becomes calmer and uncluttered with worry. With each deep breath feel yourself deepening further into quiet, alert relaxation. (pause for a few seconds)

Now imagine that you're walking down a short path through the woods…. The day is bright and sunny… feel the warm sunshine on your face… hear the birds chirping in the trees… you can smell early summer on the breeze… (pause) as you see the path take a slight turn ahead, a children's playground comes into view… stopping for a moment to see everything here… the swings… the seesaw… the sandbox… the monkey bars… the jungle gym… the merry-go-round… things to climb on… things to swing from…. A place for hopscotch… (pause)

One thing in particular draws your attention… so you walk closer and give it a try… noticing how it feels to enjoy yourself… to let go and have fun… to be free and childlike again…. (pause) looking up you notice a few of your friends coming to join you on the playground… you run over to them and begin playing a game together… laughing… enjoying the time here together… (pause) remembering what it's like to simply play… no worries… no concerns… no homework…. No stress… just spending time with friends… (pause)

After awhile you and your friends grow tired… and realize it's time to get home for dinner…. The sun is setting… the breeze turns cooler… and as you each leave the playground, you go your separate ways… (pause) you walk back down the path through the woods… thinking back to the time on the playground… feeling grateful for all the fun… promising yourself you'll do it again soon… (pause)

Gently bring your attention back to your breath. Feeling the deep inhale, exhale…. Inhale, exhale. Noticing how calm and relaxed your body feels

sitting here in this room. Gently open your awareness to this time and place, these surroundings... wiggle your fingers and toes, gently begin to move your body again.... and when you're ready, you can open your eyes.

Blowing Bubbles

Close your eyes and take some deep breaths. Feel your lungs expanding with each inhale and contracting with each exhale. Feel your body open up with each new breath. Feel your muscles relax, all tension from the day leaving your body and mind. Notice that your mind becomes calmer and uncluttered with worry. With each deep breath feel yourself deepening further into quiet, alert relaxation. (pause for a few seconds)

Now imagine that you're walking down a short path through the woods…. The day is bright and sunny… feel the warm sunshine on your face… hear the birds chirping in the trees… you can smell early summer on the breeze… (pause) as you see the path take a slight turn ahead, a children's playground comes into view… stopping for a moment to see everything here… the swings… the seesaw… the sandbox… the monkey bars… the jungle gym… the merry-go-round… things to climb on… things to swing from…. A place for hopscotch… (pause)

One thing in particular draws your attention… so you walk closer and give it a try… noticing how it feels to enjoy yourself… to let go and have fun… to be free and childlike again…. (pause) looking up you notice a few of your friends coming to join you on the playground… you run over to them and begin playing a game together… laughing… enjoying the time here together… (pause) remembering what it's like to simply play… no worries… no concerns… no homework…. No stress… just spending time with friends… (pause)

One of you notices a bottle of bubbles near the merry-go-round… picking it up, you unscrew the top and pull out the wand… see the shimmering soapy solution clinging to the wand… pucker your lips and blow… slowly the bubble appears… your friends cheer and laugh… blowing quickly, you create lots of small bubbles… watch how they form and release from the wand… how they're carried on the breeze… the rainbows inside each one… (pause) and handing the wand to a friend, you each take turns… blowing bubbles… chasing the bubbles… feeling your arms become slightly sticky when they land on you… (pause)

After awhile you and your friends grow tired… and realize it's time to get home for dinner…. The sun is setting… the breeze turns cooler… and as you each leave the playground, you go your separate ways… (pause) you walk back down the path through the woods… thinking back to the time on the playground… feeling grateful for all the fun… promising yourself you'll do it again soon… (pause)

Gently bring your attention back to your breath. Feeling the deep inhale, exhale…. Inhale, exhale. Noticing how calm and relaxed your body feels sitting here in this room. Gently open your awareness to this time and place, these surroundings… wiggle your fingers and toes, gently begin to move your body again…. and when you're ready, you can open your eyes.

Building a Fence

Close your eyes and take some deep breaths. Feel your lungs expanding with each inhale and contracting with each exhale. Feel your body open up with each new breath. Feel your muscles relax, all tension from the day leaving your body and mind. Notice that your mind becomes calmer and uncluttered with worry. With each deep breath feel yourself deepening further into quiet, alert relaxation. (pause for a few seconds)

Now imagine that you're standing outside your house... this could be the house you live in right now... or a place you've lived in the past... or a house you've visited in previous imagery experiences... using your senses, take a few moments to be aware of everything around you... (pause) the sounds... the smells... the temperature of the air... the emotions... the sights... (pause)

Looking around, you have the thought that a fence would be nice... perhaps as decoration for the yard... or perhaps as a place to plant a new flower garden... or perhaps as a boundary between your property and the neighbor's... fences keep things out... but they also keep things in... fences can define a space... provide structure... separate what's mine from what's your's... (pause) and as you're thinking these things, you notice that the materials for building your fence have appeared nearby... everything you need... (pause)

And as you begin building this fence... noticing how it feels to put it up here... how difficult or how easy it is... how it looks as it begins to take shape... how it changes the yard near your house... (pause) and continuing to build... creating it just the way you want to it be... (pause) and bringing the project to a finish for today... perhaps you've completed the fence... perhaps it needs more work... knowing you can come back whenever you want... (pause) and stepping back a moment to see what you've created here... this fence... and feeling satisfied with what you've done... taking it all in... (pause)

Feeling grateful that you could enable this amazing transformation... noticing what's changed around you... what's changed within you... you walk the way you came... feeling thankful for the time here today... for the house... for the fence... for the beauty and rest and refreshment and reflection... (pause)

Gently bring your attention back to your breath. Feeling the deep inhale, exhale.... Inhale, exhale. Noticing how calm and relaxed your body feels sitting here in this room. Gently open your awareness to this time and place, these surroundings... wiggle your fingers and toes, gently begin to move your body again.... and when you're ready, you can open your eyes.

Redecorating a House

Close your eyes and take some deep breaths. Feel your lungs expanding with each inhale and contracting with each exhale. Feel your body open up with each new breath. Feel your muscles relax, all tension from the day leaving your body and mind. Notice that your mind becomes calmer and uncluttered with worry. With each deep breath feel yourself deepening further into quiet, alert relaxation. (pause for a few seconds)

Now imagine that you're standing in front of a house... it could be a house you know... perhaps one you've lived in before... or the one you live in now... or a completely unfamiliar house to you... perhaps one you've always wanted to live in... (pause) Notice how it appears on the outside... its' size and shape... its' color... all the details of its' exterior... perhaps even the landscaping surrounding it... (pause) Notice what is beautiful here... notice what you'd like to change... (pause)

And now walking up to the front door... and entering the house... notice the inside... the room you first enter... be aware of the details... the size and shape... the furnishings... the colors... the atmosphere... (pause) pass on to another room and notice the details here as well.... (pause) and another room... and on through the house... paying close attention to what is beautiful here... and what you would change... (pause)

After walking through the entire house, you make your way back to something... and object... or a room... or a piece of furniture... or a decoration... something that you wanted to change... find your way back to that... and begin to make that change... (pause) maybe the wall needs a different color of paint... or the furniture needs rearranging... or fresh flowers need to be on a table... or pictures on the wall need updating... whatever it is, begin making that change... (long pause)

And when you have finished, step back and admire your work... how beautiful it is... and notice how that change effects everything else... (pause) and feeling satisfied with what you've done, you make your way through the house again... and out the front door... and back outside... standing again in front of the house... admiring it... knowing that this is your house... and you can return whenever you wish... perhaps simply to enjoy time away here... perhaps to make more changes... (pause)

Feeling grateful that you could enable this amazing transformation... noticing what's changed around you... what's changed within you... you walk the way you came... feeling thankful for the time here today... for the house... for the beauty and rest and refreshment and reflection... (pause)

Gently bring your attention back to your breath. Feeling the deep inhale, exhale.... Inhale, exhale. Noticing how calm and relaxed your body feels sitting here in this room. Gently open your awareness to this time and place, these surroundings... wiggle your fingers and toes, gently begin to move your body again.... and when you're ready, you can open your eyes.

Rainbow

Close your eyes and take some deep breaths. Feel your lungs expanding with each inhale and contracting with each exhale. Feel your body open up with each new breath. Feel your muscles relax, all tension from the day leaving your body and mind. Notice that your mind becomes calmer and uncluttered with worry. With each deep breath feel yourself deepening further into quiet, alert relaxation. (pause for a few seconds)

Now imagine that you're walking down a short path through the woods.... Notice the trees and plants around you... hear the sounds of birds nearby... see the vibrant colors of flowers blooming... feel the worn path beneath your feet... the temperature of the air against your skin... using all your senses to experience this walk in the woods... (pause)

As you inhale a deep breath of forest air, you notice the scent of rain... straining your ears you can just begin to hear the sound of raindrops hitting the leaves overhead... quietly and slowly at first... gradually gaining in frequency... until you're caught in a rain shower... (pause) noticing a large tree nearby, you jog over to take shelter under its' canopy... standing next to the massive trunk you look up into the branches and limbs... straight towards the top... watching as a few raindrops filter through and fall down... (pause)

Standing there next to the tree trunk, you imagine the rainwater nourishing the ground below... rejuvenating the plants and trees with its' nourishment.... giving them life... helping them grow.... refreshing everything here... (pause)

Looking through the leaves, you notice a glimpse of color... stepping out from under the canopy of the tree you can see more clearly that a rainbow has formed... you marvel at the full spectrum of colors in it... (pause) and as you look at it, it appears to be getting larger... you realize that somehow it's actually moving towards you... taking a few steps forward brings you directly into the midst of the rainbow... you can see the many colors on your hands and arms… and for those few moments before the rainbow moves on… you are the treasure at the end of the rainbow… you… (pause)

After awhile you hear the rain begin to slow down… noticing what's changed around you… what's changed within you… the sun is setting… the breeze turns cooler… you walk back down the path through the woods… feeling grateful for the time here today… for the rain… for the trees… for the rest and refreshment… for the rainbow… (pause)

Gently bring your attention back to your breath. Feeling the deep inhale, exhale…. Inhale, exhale. Noticing how calm and relaxed your body feels sitting here in this room. Gently open your awareness to this time and place, these surroundings… wiggle your fingers and toes, gently begin to move your body again…. and when you're ready, you can open your eyes.

Author's Note: This script is a bit different than the others in the book. It was created to offer options for your group/individual based on the intent for the session. If your focus falls into one of these particular areas, then this script might be interesting to use with participants. The beginning and ending portions are meant to be read every time you use this script, but the portions in italics are your options. For example, you would read the beginning, then jump to "prosperity," and then finish up with the ending portion. This could be especially useful if you find that certain themes or topics are regularly coming up in your group/individual sessions, or if participants are stating that they have an interest in exploring these specific areas.

Magic Water Fountain

Close your eyes and take some deep breaths. Feel your lungs expanding with each inhale and contracting with each exhale. Feel your body open up with each new breath. Feel your muscles relax, all tension from the day leaving your body and mind. Notice that your mind becomes calmer and uncluttered with worry. With each deep breath feel yourself deepening further into quiet, alert relaxation. (pause for a few seconds)

Now imagine that you're standing in a lush garden... beautiful flowers and plants all around you... notice their vibrant colors... the fragrant aromas... the many different varieties of flowers and blooms.... (pause) You walk slowly through the garden, enjoying the peaceful feeling of being here amongst all the growth... (pause) After several moments of walking, you notice ahead of you a water fountain in the center of the garden... you walk closer to get a better look... notice it's size... and shape... how the water flows... how the air temperature changes slightly as you get closer... the sound of the water... (pause) As you walk around the fountain, you notice a small metal signpost nearby... getting closer, you see that it says "Magic Water Fountain"... You reach out to touch the sign and accidentally bump it so that it turns over to the backside...

Health:
it says "health"... you think about the current state of your physical health... your emotional health... your mental health... your spiritual health... your relationship health... and you imagine how each of those areas could change and improve... (pause) dipping your fingers into the water at the base of the fountain, you're surprised at how wonderful it feels.... You find a place to sit comfortably next to the fountain... letting your fingers play in the water... noticing how the water feels... mesmerized by observing the water... how it moves through your fingers... (pause) after a few minutes of this, you notice that you feel better... it's difficult to pinpoint exactly where... or how... only that you notice your thoughts are lighter... your breathing easier... your muscles more relaxed... your spirit somehow renewed... (pause) and now when you think of the areas of health in your life, you have a sense of optimism... of hopefulness... breathing deeply be keenly aware of how that feels... (pause)

Prosperity:
It says "prosperity"... you think about what that means to you... in areas of money... relationships... personal worth... creativity... and you imagine how each of those areas could change and improve... (pause) dipping your fingers into the water at the base of the fountain, you're surprised at how wonderful it feels.... You find a place to sit comfortably next to the fountain... letting your fingers play in the water... noticing how the water feels... mesmerized by observing the water... how it moves through your fingers... (pause) after a few minutes of this, you notice that you feel better... it's difficult to pinpoint exactly where... or how... only that you notice your thoughts are lighter... your breathing easier... your muscles more relaxed... your spirit somehow renewed... (pause) and now when you think of the areas of prosperity in your life, you have a sense of optimism... of hopefulness... breathing deeply be keenly aware of how that feels... (pause)

Time:
it says "time"... you think about what that means to you... time management... lifetime... free time... lack of time... or too much time... making the most of your time... and you imagine how each of those areas could change and improve... (pause) dipping your fingers into the water at the base of the fountain, you're surprised at how wonderful it feels.... You find a place to sit comfortably next to the fountain... letting your fingers play in the water... noticing how the water feels... mesmerized by observing the water... how it moves through your fingers... (pause) after a few minutes of this, you notice that you feel better... it's difficult to pinpoint exactly where... or how... only that you notice your thoughts are lighter... your breathing easier... your muscles more relaxed... your spirit somehow renewed... (pause) and now when you think of the areas of time in your life, you have a sense of optimism... of hopefulness... breathing deeply be keenly aware of how that feels... (pause)

Youth:
It says "youth"... you think about what that means to you... a fountain of youth... what would you want from it?... need from it?... and you imagine how each of those areas could change and improve... (pause) dipping your fingers into the water at the base of the fountain, you're surprised at how wonderful it feels.... You find a place to sit comfortably next to the fountain... letting your fingers play in the water... noticing how the water feels... mesmerized by observing the water... how it moves through your fingers... (pause) after a few minutes of this, you notice that you feel better... it's difficult to pinpoint exactly where... or how... only that you notice your thoughts are lighter... your breathing easier... your muscles more relaxed... your spirit somehow renewed... (pause) and now when you think of the idea of youthfulness in your life, you have a sense of optimism... of hopefulness... breathing deeply be keenly aware of how that feels... (pause)

Wisdom:
It says "wisdom"... you think about what that means to you... knowledge... intuition... deeper understanding... broader awareness...

and you imagine how each of those areas could change and improve... (pause) dipping your fingers into the water at the base of the fountain, you're surprised at how wonderful it feels.... You find a place to sit comfortably next to the fountain... letting your fingers play in the water... noticing how the water feels... mesmerized by observing the water... how it moves through your fingers... (pause) after a few minutes of this, you notice that you feel better... it's difficult to pinpoint exactly where... or how... only that you notice your thoughts are lighter... your breathing easier... your muscles more relaxed... your spirit somehow renewed... (pause) and now when you think of the idea of wisdom in your life, you have a sense of optimism... of hopefulness... breathing deeply be keenly aware of how that feels... (pause)

Regrets:
It says "regrets"... you think about what that means to you... past regrets... current regrets... relationships and life events you wish had been or could be different... and you imagine how each of those areas could change and improve... (pause) dipping your fingers into the water at the base of the fountain, you're surprised at how wonderful it feels.... You find a place to sit comfortably next to the fountain... letting your fingers play in the water... noticing how the water feels... mesmerized by observing the water... how it moves through your fingers... (pause) after a few minutes of this, you notice that you feel better... it's difficult to pinpoint exactly where... or how... only that you notice your thoughts are lighter... your breathing easier... your muscles more relaxed... your spirit somehow renewed... (pause) and now when you think of the areas of regrets in your life, you have a sense of optimism... of hopefulness... breathing deeply be keenly aware of how that feels... (pause)

Standing up next to the fountain, you feel a sense of gratitude for these moments spent here.... Learning more about yourself... gaining insight... (pause) and with that feeling of thankfulness you being to walk back through the garden... smelling the flowers... feeling the warm air... noticing the bright sunlight.... (pause)

Gently bring your attention back to your breath. Feeling the deep inhale, exhale…. Inhale, exhale. Noticing how calm and relaxed your body feels sitting here in this room. Gently open your awareness to this time and place, these surroundings… wiggle your fingers and toes, gently begin to move your body again…. and when you're ready, you can open your eyes.

Deeper Wisdom

Scripts

Riverbank with Rocks

Close your eyes and take some deep breaths. Feel your lungs expanding with each inhale and contracting with each exhale. Feel your body open up with each new breath. Feel your muscles relax, all tension from the day leaving your body and mind. Notice that your mind becomes calmer and uncluttered with worry. With each deep breath feel yourself deepening further into quiet, alert relaxation. (pause for a few seconds)

Now imagine that you're standing on a riverbank. Notice how the river looks…. is it a wide river or a smaller one… Is it running fast or slow… is the water clear or murky… deep or shallow…. can you see any fish swimming by…. Notice how the water moves…. Hear the sounds of the water gently lapping against the riverbank nearby….

As you're looking at your surroundings, your attention is drawn to a pile of rocks nearby on the riverbank… you move closer to examine them…. Picking them up one at a time you notice how each one is slightly different…. Look at their different colors… shapes…. Sizes…. Textures…. As you examine each one you begin to notice that there is writing on them… read what they say…. (long pause here)… after you've spent time reading the messages, choose the one that you need to hear the most… spend a few moments studying that rock… taking in that message…. (pause here)

Feeling like you've absorbed what you need from this experience with the rocks, you slip your rock into your pocket and bring it back with you… you begin walking back the way you came… noticing if anything about your surroundings is different…. Notice if you feel different…. Thinking about what you've learned here today…. (short pause here)

Gently bring your attention back to your breath. Feeling the deep inhale, exhale…. Inhale, exhale. Noticing how calm and relaxed your body feels

sitting here in this room. Gently open your awareness to this time and place, these surroundings... wiggle your fingers and toes, gently begin to move your body again.... and when you're ready, you can open your eyes.

Messages on Stones

Close your eyes and take some deep breaths. Feel your lungs expanding with each inhale and contracting with each exhale. Feel your body open up with each new breath. Feel your muscles relax, all tension from the day leaving your body and mind. Notice that your mind becomes calmer and uncluttered with worry. With each deep breath feel yourself deepening further into quiet, alert relaxation. (pause for a few seconds)

Now imagine that you're standing on a riverbank. Notice how the river looks…. is it a wide river or a smaller one… Is it running fast or slow… is the water clear or murky… deep or shallow…. can you see any fish swimming by…. Notice how the water moves…. Hear the sounds of the water gently lapping against the riverbank nearby….

As you're looking at your surroundings, your attention is drawn to a pile of stones nearby on the riverbank… you move closer to examine them…. Picking them up one at a time you notice how each one is slightly different…. Look at their different colors… shapes…. Sizes…. Textures…. Just at the edge of your eyesight you notice something glimmering under a leaf… looking closer you see that it's a gold writing pen… picking it up you use it to write a message on one of the stones…. Something you want to release… something you want to let go of… you pick up another stone and do the same…. Picking up as many stones as you need to… letting go of what needs to be released…. (pause here)… once you've written all you need to, you pick up each stone one by one and toss them into the river… feeling a sense of release with each one…. Feeling yourself grow lighter and more free each time…. (long pause here)

Feeling like you've absorbed what you need from this experience with the stones … you begin walking back the way you came… noticing if anything about your surroundings is different…. Notice if you feel different…. Thinking about what you've learned here today…. (short pause here)

Gently bring your attention back to your breath. Feeling the deep inhale, exhale…. Inhale, exhale. Noticing how calm and relaxed your body feels sitting here in this room. Gently open your awareness to this time and place, these surroundings… wiggle your fingers and toes, gently begin to move your body again…. and when you're ready, you can open your eyes.

Decluttering the Attic

Close your eyes and take some deep breaths. Feel your lungs expanding with each inhale and contracting with each exhale. Feel your body open up with each new breath. Feel your muscles relax, all tension from the day leaving your body and mind. Notice that your mind becomes calmer and uncluttered with worry. With each deep breath feel yourself deepening further into quiet, alert relaxation. (pause for a few seconds)

Now imagine that you're standing in front of a set of stairs... the stairs are rather steep but easily manageable for you... you begin climbing and soon emerge into an attic space... flipping a light switch nearby you notice what's around you here... become aware of what this space feels like... how it smells... the air around you.... (pause) You notice an item close by that you no longer need... so you set it aside to throw away later... and think to yourself that there are probably other things up here you no longer need... that are of no use to you anymore... and you begin to look through what has been stored away up here... looking for those things you can release... let go... get rid of.... (long pause) As you find these things to release, you set them aside... in a pile all their own... (long pause)

When you have done enough for today, you gather up what's in the pile to be released.... You stop for a moment to consider how to let go of these things... what's a fitting way to do that... (pause) and once you've decided, you go about the work of releasing them... one by one.... (pause) letting go.... Of things you no longer need... of patterns that no longer serve you... of emotions that hold you back... releasing them... (pause)

Breathing deeply... feeling the shift in yourself after letting go... becoming more comfortable in the new space within... bringing with you a deep sense of relaxation... peace... calm...

Gently bring your attention back to your breath. Feeling the deep inhale, exhale.... Inhale, exhale. Noticing how calm and relaxed your body feels sitting here in this room. Gently open your awareness to this time and place, these surroundings… wiggle your fingers and toes, gently begin to move your body again…. and when you're ready, you can open your eyes.

Inner Wisdom

Close your eyes and take some deep breaths. Feel your lungs expanding with each inhale and contracting with each exhale. Feel your body open up with each new breath. Feel your muscles relax, all tension from the day leaving your body and mind. Notice that your mind becomes calmer and uncluttered with worry. With each deep breath feel yourself deepening further into quiet, alert relaxation. (pause for a few seconds)

Become aware of how it feels to breathe in…. and out…. (pause) notice if the air changes temperature slightly as you inhale and exhale… pay attention to the smallest detail… (pause) now bringing your attention to how the air fills your lungs… and leaves your lungs…. (pause) notice how your body changes slightly to accommodate each inhale… and exhale… how your chest expands… how your belly expands… and how they relax… (pause) until you're fully… deeply… effortlessly breathing… (pause)

Now following your breath inward…. Feeling that inner space expanding with each breath… this space is a place of deep knowledge… wisdom… insight… and we all have this space inside… we can access this place through breathing… and focusing… and resting here from time to time… (pause) Notice how this space feels… its' expansiveness… its' depth of knowledge… relax for a moment here… listening intently… attuning to what it may have to share with you…. What wisdom is here for you today… (long pause)

Taking in that message… accepting the wisdom… allowing it to really sink in… (pause) feeling grateful for this time here in this space… and knowing you can return whenever you wish… to this place that resides deep within yourself… (pause)

Gently bring your attention back to your breath. Feeling the deep inhale, exhale…. Inhale, exhale. Noticing how calm and relaxed your body feels

sitting here in this room. Gently open your awareness to this time and place, these surroundings… wiggle your fingers and toes, gently begin to move your body again…. and when you're ready, you can open your eyes.

Treasure Box

Close your eyes and take some deep breaths. Feel your lungs expanding with each inhale and contracting with each exhale. Feel your body open up with each new breath. Feel your muscles relax, all tension from the day leaving your body and mind. Notice that your mind becomes calmer and uncluttered with worry. With each deep breath feel yourself deepening further into quiet, alert relaxation. (pause for a few seconds)

Now imagine that you're walking outside in nature…. It can be anywhere you choose… a familiar place… or a new place…. Feel the temperature of the air around you… inhale deeply the scent of the outdoors… hear the sound of birds… notice the colors of everything around you… feel the ground beneath your feet… (pause) enjoy the feeling of not being rushed or hurried… knowing you can take as much time as you want here… (pause)

As you're walking, you stop to take a closer look at some of the flowers and bushes nearby… noticing their vibrant colors… their aromas… the way in which they grow… and as you're looking at them, you notice something mostly hidden by the leaves of a bush… taking a closer look, you see that it's a box… pulling it out you examine it… its' weight… its' decorations… and finding a latch, you open the top… inside it's empty except for a pencil and paper… sitting down next to where you found it, you decide to write a message to your future Self… some wisdom or a lesson learned… or maybe you're rather leave a gift… you take a few moments to do so… (long pause)

After your task is complete and you feel like you've done what you need to, you place your message or gift inside the box and close it up… placing it back where you found it… noticing what's changed around you… what's changed within you… the sun is setting… the breeze turns cooler… you walk the way you came… feeling grateful for the time here today… for the walk… for the box… for the rest and refreshment and reflection… (pause)

Gently bring your attention back to your breath. Feeling the deep inhale, exhale…. Inhale, exhale. Noticing how calm and relaxed your body feels sitting here in this room. Gently open your awareness to this time and place, these surroundings… wiggle your fingers and toes, gently begin to move your body again…. and when you're ready, you can open your eyes.

Wise Person

Close your eyes and take some deep breaths. Feel your lungs expanding with each inhale and contracting with each exhale. Feel your body open up with each new breath. Feel your muscles relax, all tension from the day leaving your body and mind. Notice that your mind becomes calmer and uncluttered with worry. With each deep breath feel yourself deepening further into quiet, alert relaxation. (pause for a few seconds)

Now imagine that you're standing in front of a door… see the door clearly in your mind… notice its' shape… the material it's made of… its' color… reach out to turn the doorknob and open the door…. On the other side you find a spacious porch… stepping through the door you look around and observe the surroundings… what do you see? (pause) Notice the temperature of the air…. The sounds you hear… does this place seem familiar, or is it new to you? Using all of your senses to experience this place… (pause)

Your attention is drawn to a pair of rocking chairs on the far end of the porch… walking over to one, you sit down and begin slowly rocking… back and forth… back and forth… feeling the gentle motion of the chair as it moves… how relaxing it feels to simply sit and rock…. Observing your surroundings on the porch… feeling comfortable here… simply watching what happens around you… enjoying this time to yourself to relax and be still…. (long pause)

You hear footsteps approaching from nearby and look over to see someone coming… this person greets you warmly and sits next to you in the other rocking chair… rocking together quietly for a few moments… this person says they have a message for you… some wisdom to share… you listen eagerly and receptively to what they have to say… (pause) perhaps you talk about it… perhaps you simply sit in easy companionship… letting the message sink in… (long pause)

After awhile you sense a shift in the temperature and realize that the day will be coming to a close soon... letting the rocking chair slowly stop moving... savoring these last few moments on the porch with this person... (pause) smiling at the person and expressing your thanks to them, you rise from the chair and walk along the porch to the door... opening it back up... crossing over the threshold... bringing with you a deep sense of relaxation... peace... calm... wisdom...

Gently bring your attention back to your breath. Feeling the deep inhale, exhale.... Inhale, exhale. Noticing how calm and relaxed your body feels sitting here in this room. Gently open your awareness to this time and place, these surroundings... wiggle your fingers and toes, gently begin to move your body again.... and when you're ready, you can open your eyes.

List of Suggested Music for Scripts

This is by no means an exhaustive list of music for you to use with the scripts. Consider it merely a starting place for your own experimentation. Try these pieces, see what fits, and determine which work best for yourself and your groups. Most of the suggested pieces are approximately 5-10 minutes in length. This is to allow for varying script lengths and the needs of your particular group in each experience.

There are several ways in which to use the music—play one piece per script (either once through or repeated until your group experience is concluded) or create your own 'mini-program' of 2-3 pieces to accompany a particular script. The music can be faded in/out at the beginning and end of the group experience as needed, or the music could begin at a certain point into the script and play through to the end. Be flexible and creative, and adjust the music to fit the needs of your group. None of this is written in stone, and there is no 'right/wrong' way to go about using the music. There is simply the way that fits the session for today.

George Winston "Plains" CD
George Winston "Autumn" CD
George Winston "December" CD
George Winston "Forest" CD
Secret Garden "Red Moon" CD
Peter Kater & Carlos Nakai "Migration" CD
Peter Kater & Carlos Nakai "Through Windows and Walls" CD
Paul Winter "Sunsinger" CD
Liz Story "Speechless" CD
Liz Story "17 Seconds to Anywhere" CD
Liz Story "Solid Colors" CD
Michael Hoppe "Solace" CD
Michael Hoppe "Unforgetting Heart" CD

Daniel Kobialka "Short on Perfection" CD
Daniel Kobialka "Dreams Beyond Twilight" CD
Narada Collection Series "A Childhood Remembered" CD
Ralph Vaughan Williams Symphony #3 "Pastoral", 2nd movement
Ralph Vaughan Williams Symphony #2 "London Symphony", 2nd movement

Creative Adaptations for Sessions

Questions to ask:

- What part of the experience stands out most to you?
- What part of the experience seems most meaningful?
- What part of the experience seems most puzzling?
- Did you encounter any person, place, sense, or emotion that was familiar?
- Did you encounter any person, place, sense, or emotion that was uncomfortable?
- Did you encounter any person, place, sense, or emotion that was surprising?
- Was there something you were hoping to experience but didn't?
- How do you feel now compared to before the imagery experience began?
- What was something important you learned from this experience?
- Will anything change as a result of your experience?
- If you came today with a specific intent or problem to address, how did the imagery experience help you with that?

Activities for deepening the experience:

- Create mandalas related to the imagery
- Songwriting to reflect the experience
- Partner with an aromatherapist to pair essential oils with the session intent
- Journal writing
- Create a collage from magazine pictures reflecting the imagery
- Drumming
- Partner with a yoga teacher for a more body-focused experience
- Write out the imagery experience 'scrapbook style' with illustrations and comments on fancy paper

- Use modeling clay to create something that illustrates the experience
- Make a playlist of songs that reflect the imagery
- Partner with a Reiki practitioner to enhance the energy experience

Additional suggestions:

- Improvise live music during the imagery experience
- Use Tibetan or crystal singing bowls during the imagery experience

Resources

Bonny, Helen & Savary, Louis. *Music & Your Mind: Listening with a New Consciousness.* (2011). Barcelona Publishers: Gilsum, NH.

Bruscia, Kenneth E. & Grocke, Denise E. (eds.) *Guided Imagery and Music: The Bonny Method and Beyond.* (2002). Barcelona Publishers: Gilsum, NH.

Bush, Carol. A. *Healing Imagery & Music: Pathways to the Inner Self.* (1995). MMB Music: St. Louis, MO.

Cantello, Matthew. *Communing with Music: Practicing the Art of Conscious Listening.* (2004). DeVorss & Co.: Camarillo, CA.

About the Author

Stephanie Bolton is a master's level board certified music therapist, Fellow of the Association for Music and Imagery, and owner of Healing Sounds Music Therapy, a private practice in north Alabama specializing in guided imagery and music techniques. Her clients are primarily adults seeking to manage mental health issues, overcome health challenges, improve difficult relationships, or simply enhance their emotional wellbeing. She also offers professional music therapy supervision.

Check out her website and blog at
www.imageryandmusic.com.

Check out her previous book
Diving Deeper: 30 Guided Visualization Scripts
For Individual and Group Work.

Printed in Great Britain
by Amazon